LIVES
AND
TIMES

Beatrix Potter

Jayne Woodhouse

Heinemann
LIBRARY

First published in Great Britain by Heinemann Library
Halley Court, Jordan Hill, Oxford OX2 8EJ,
a division of Reed Educational and Professional Publishing Ltd.
Heinemann is a registered trademark of Reed Educational & Professional Publishing Limited.

OXFORD FLORENCE PRAGUE MADRID ATHENS
MELBOURNE AUCKLAND KUALA LUMPUR SINGAPORE TOKYO
IBADAN NAIROBI KAMPALA JOHANNESBURG GABORONE
PORTSMOUTH NH (USA) CHICAGO MEXICO CITY SAO PAULO

Designed by Ken Vail Graphic Design, Cambridge
Illustrations by Alice Englander
Printed in Hong Kong / China

02 01 00 99
10 9 8 7 6 5 4 3 2 1

ISBN 0 431 02492 8 (This title is also available in a hardback library edition ISBN 0 43102485 5)

Some words are shown in bold, **like this**. You can find out what they mean by looking in the glossary. The glossary also helps you say difficult words.

British Library Cataloguing in Publication Data

Woodhouse, Jayne
Beatrix Potter. - (Lives & times)
1. Potter, Beatrix, 1866–1943 - Juvenile literature 2. Women novelists,
English - 20th century - Biography - Juvenile literature
I. Title
823 .9'12

Acknowledgements

Illustrations and photographs on pages 16, 17, 21, 22, 23 copyright © Frederick Warne & Co., 1901, 1908, 1946, 1987. Photographs on pages 18, 19 courtesy of the Victoria & Albert Museum. Photographs on pages 20, 21 courtesy of the National Trust Photographic Library. Cover photograph courtesy of the Victoria & Albert Museum. Reproduced by kind permission of Frederick Warne & Co.

Our thanks to Betty Root for her comments in the preparation of this book. Every effort has been made to contact copyright holders of any material reproduced in this book. Any omissions will be rectified in subsequent printings if notice is given to the Publisher.

Frederick Warne & Co. is the owner of all rights, copyrights and trademarks in the Beatrix Potter character names and illustrations.

Contents

The first part of this book tells you the story of
Beatrix Potter.
The second part tells you how we can find out
about her life.

Who is Beatrix Potter?

Have you heard of Peter Rabbit, Jemima Puddle-duck and Squirrel Nutkin? You will find them all in little books written by the same **author**. Her name is Beatrix Potter.

Beatrix Potter was born in London in
1866. Her parents were rich. They lived
in a big house and had servants to look
after them.

Childhood

Beatrix was a very lonely girl. She wasn't allowed to have any friends and she didn't go to school. A **governess** taught her at home on her own.

Beatrix's friends were her pets. She kept mice, snails, bats, hedgehogs, frogs, lizards and rabbits.

A young artist

Beatrix loved to draw and paint. She spent hours watching her animals and drawing them. Her pictures were very good.

When Beatrix grew up, she had to stay at home to look after her parents. She was often bored and sad. Her happiest times were her holidays in the countryside or the time she spent painting.

The letter

When Beatrix was 27, she wrote a special letter to a little boy who was ill. It told him a story about a rabbit called Peter. It had lots of her own pictures.

Then Beatrix thought, 'Perhaps some other children would like to read this story.' She made the letter into a book and drew a picture for each page. She called it *The Tale of Peter Rabbit*.

The book

Beatrix sent the book to six **publishers.**
They didn't like it and sent it back. At last,
a publisher called Frederick Warne & Co.
said they would publish it.

Children loved *Peter Rabbit*. 'You must write more books,' said the publisher. Now Beatrix had found a way to use her painting skills and her love of animals.

Marriage

Beatrix always loved the countryside. With the money from her books, she bought a farm in the Lake District. It was called Hill Top. When she was 47, she married William Heelis who lived nearby.

Soon Beatrix stopped writing books. She began to buy and look after more farms. People forgot that Mrs Heelis was once Beatrix Potter, the famous author. She died when she was 77.

Her books

It is nearly 100 years since Beatrix Potter wrote *The Tale of Peter Rabbit*, but children today still love her stories. They are published in many different languages and in **braille**.

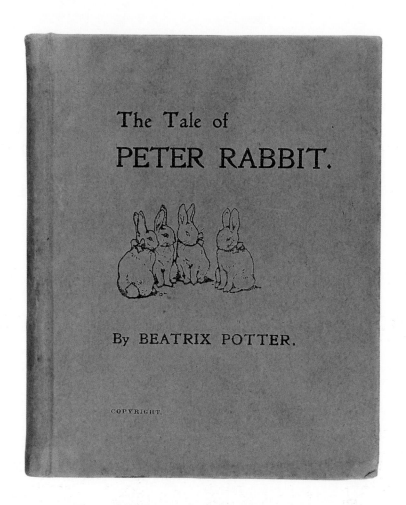

Beatrix was asked how she thought of stories that children would enjoy. 'I have just made stories to please myself,' she said, 'because I never grew up.'

Photographs

Photographs of Beatrix Potter show us what she looked like at different times in her life.

Buildings

Beatrix's house, Hill Top, is now a **museum**. Inside you can see how she lived. Her furniture, pictures, ornaments and clothes are still there.

Beatrix wrote many of her books at Hill Top. You can see parts of the farmhouse in her pictures.

Writing

This is a page from Beatrix's secret **diary**. It is written in **code**. The code was broken a long time after she died. The diary tells us many things about her life.

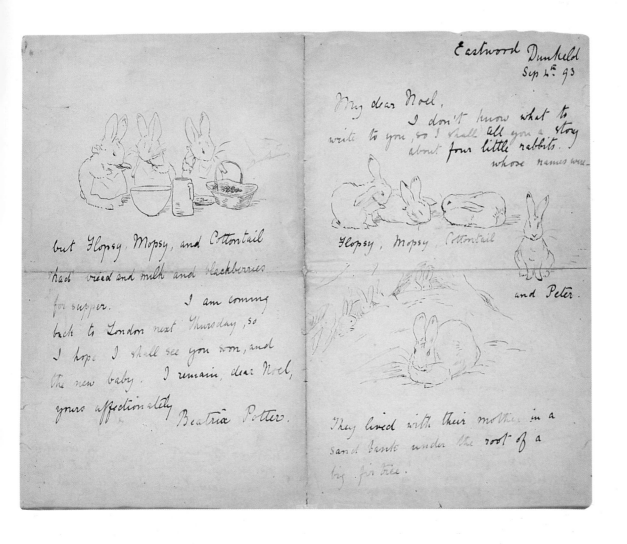

Beatrix's picture letter about Peter Rabbit still exists. Can you read the beginning of the story?

Glossary

This glossary explains difficult words, and helps you to say words which are hard to say.

author a person who writes books
You say *or-ther*

braille a special kind of writing, that you feel, for the blind to read, invented by Louis Braille.
You say *brale*

code a special way of writing that stops most people from understanding what you have written

diary where you write what happens to you or what you are thinking about, day by day

governess a woman who teaches children at their home

museum a building which contains objects that tell us about science, art or history

publisher someone who turns writing into books

Index